SOME MAJOR EVENTS IN WORLD WAR II

THE EUROPEAN THEATER

1939 SEPTEMBER—Germany invades Poland Great Britain, France, Australia, & New Zealand declare war on Germany; Battle of the Atlantic begins. NOVEMBER—Russia invades Finland.

1940 APRIL—Germany invades Denmark & Norway. MAY—Germany invades Belgium, Luxembourg, & The Netherlands; British forces retreat to Dunkirk and escape to England. JUNE—Italy declares war on Britain & France; France surrenders to Germany. JULY—Battle of Britain begins. SEPTEMBER—Italy invades Egypt; Germany, Italy, & Japan form the Axis countries. OCTOBER—Italy invades Greece. NOVEMBER—Battle of Britain over. DECEMBER—Britain attacks Italy in North Africa.

1941 JANUARY—Allies take Tobruk. FEBRUARY—Rommel arrives at Tripoli. APRIL—Germany invades Greece & Yugoslavia. JUNE—Allies are in Syria; Germany invades Russia. JULY—Russia joins Allies. AUGUST—Germans capture Kiev. OCTOBER—Germany reaches Moscow. DECEMBER—Germans retreat from Moscow; Japan attacks Pearl Harbor; United States enters war against Axis nations.

1942 MAY—first British bomber attack on Cologne. JUNE—Germans take Tobruk. SEPTEMBER—Battle of Stalingrad begins. OCTOBER—Battle of El Alamein begins. NOVEMBER—Allies recapture Tobruk; Russians counterattack at Stalingrad.

1943 JANUARY—Allies take Tripoli. FEBRUARY—German troops at Stalingrad surrender. APRIL—revolt of Warsaw Ghetto Jews begins. MAY—German and Italian resistance in North Africa is over; their troops surrender in Tunisia; Warsaw Ghetto revolt is put down by Germany. JULY—allies invade Sicily; Mussolini put in prison. SEPTEMBER—Allies land in Italy; Italians surrender; Germans occupy Rome; Mussolini rescued by Germany. OCTOBER—Allies capture Naples; Italy declares war on Germany. NOVEMBER—Russians recapture Kiev.

1944 JANUARY—Allies land at Anzio. JUNE—Rome falls to Allies; Allies land in Normandy (D-Day). JULY—assassination attempt on Hitler fails. AUGUST—Allies land in southern France. SEPTEMBER—Brussels freed. OCTOBER—Athens liberated. DECEMBER—Battle of the Bulge.

1945 JANUARY—Russians free Warsaw. FEBRUARY—Dresden bombed. APRIL—Americans take Belsen and Buchenwald concentration camps; Russians free Vienna; Russians take over Berlin; Mussolini killed; Hitler commits suicide. MAY—Germany surrenders; Goering captured.

THE PACIFIC THEATER

1940 SEPTEMBER—Japan joins Axis nations Germany & Italy.

1941 APRIL—Russia & Japan sign neutrality pact. DECEMBER—Japanese launch attacks against Pearl Harbor, Hong Kong, the Philippines, & Malaya; United States and Allied nations declare war on Japan; China declares war on Japan, Germany, & Italy; Japan takes over Guam, Wake Island, & Hong Kong; Japan attacks Burma.

1942 JANUARY—Japan takes over Manila; Japan invades Dutch East Indies. FEBRUARY—Japan takes over Singapore; Battle of the Java Sea. APRIL—Japanese overrun Bataan. MAY—Japan takes Mandalay; Allied forces in Philippines surrender to Japan; Japan takes Corregidor; Battle of the Coral Sea. JUNE—Battle of Midway; Japan occupies Aleutian Islands. AUGUST—United States invades Guadalcanal in the Solomon Islands.

1943 FEBRUARY—Guadalcanal taken by U.S. Marines. MARCH—Japanese begin to retreat in China. APRIL—Yamamoto shot down by U.S. Air Force. MAY—U.S. troops take Aleutian Islands back from Japan. JUNE—Allied troops land in New Guinea. NOVEMBER—U.S. Marines invade Bougainville & Tarawa.

1944 FEBRUARY—Truk liberated. JUNE—Saipan attacked by United States. JULY—battle for Guam begins. OCTOBER—U.S. troops invade Philippines; Battle of Leyte Gulf won by Allies.

1945 JANUARY—Luzon taken; Burma Road won back. MARCH—Iwo Jima freed. APRIL—Okinawa attacked by U.S. troops; President Franklin Roosevelt dies; Harry S. Truman becomes president. JUNE—United States takes Okinawa. AUGUST—atomic bomb dropped on Hiroshima; Russia declares war on Japan; atomic bomb dropped on Nagasaki. SEPTEMBER—Japan surrenders.

WORLD AT WAR

Battle of
Guadalcanal

WORLD AT WAR

Battle of Guadalcanal

By R. Conrad Stein

Consultant:
    Professor Robert L. Messer, Ph.D.
    Department of History
    University of Illinois at Chicago

ℚℙ CHILDRENS PRESS, CHICAGO

The Japanese enjoyed great success in the early days of the war.
This picture was taken from a Japanese soldier who was captured
by United States Marines on Guadalcanal.

FRONTISPIECE: A Marine
observation post on Guadalcanal

Library of Congress Cataloging in Publication Data

Stein, R. Conrad.
  Battle of Guadalcanal.

  (World at war)
  Includes index.
  Summary: Describes the bloody, three-month-long
battle of U.S. Marines and Japanese troops for control
of Guadalcanal, part of the Solomon Islands located
between Hawaii and Australia.
  1. World War, 1939–1945—Campaigns—
Solomon Islands—Guadalcanal Island—Juvenile
literature.
2. Guadalcanal Island (Solomon Islands)—
History— Juvenile literature. [1. World War,
1939–1945—Campaigns—Solomon
Islands—Guadalcanal Island.
2. Guadalcanal Island (Solomon Islands)—
History] I. Title. II. Series.
D767.98.S74 1983   940.54′26   82-17883
ISBN 0-516-04771-X

  4 5 6 7 8 9 10 R 91 90 89 88 87 86

PICTURE CREDITS:
UPI: Cover, pages 4, 6, 10, 11, 12, 13
(top and left), 14, 15, 16 (top), 17, 18,
19. 20, 23, 24, 26, 27, 29, 33, 35 (right),
36, 37, 38, 39, 40, 41, 42, 46
WIDE WORLD PHOTOS: Pages 13
(bottom right), 16 (bottom), 31, 32, 35
(left), 45
Len Meents (Map): Page 9

COVER PHOTO: After blasting out
the well-entrenched Japanese, United
States Marines marched through the
fire-blackened remains of the village of
Matanikou on the island of
Guadalcanal.

PROJECT EDITOR:
Joan Downing

CREATIVE DIRECTOR:
Margrit Fiddle

After their attack on Pearl Harbor on December 7, 1941, the Japanese enjoyed a glorious string of conquests in the Pacific. They drove their enemies out of the Philippines, Malaya, Burma, Guam, and Wake Island. Many Japanese military men believed their armies were invincible. So, with great confidence, they began taking over the jungle-covered islands called the Solomons.

The Solomon Islands lay in the sea-lanes running between Hawaii and Australia. Few of the islands were occupied by Allied troops. But the Australian government was aware of the importance of the Solomons. Groups of "coastwatchers" had been organized there. The coastwatchers were Australian and British people who lived on the outlying islands. Some were coconut growers, others were traders, still others were loners who preferred life in the jungle to English civilization. The coastwatchers used secret radios to report Japanese troop and ship movements. In May of 1942, one coastwatcher sent the shocking news that the Japanese had begun construction of an airstrip on Guadalcanal, one of the Solomon Islands.

Guadalcanal is an island about ninety miles long and thirty miles wide. Nowhere on the island can one find a canal. The island was called Guadalcanal in 1568 by a Spanish explorer who named it after a town in Spain.

Worried Allied commanders discussed the airfield construction on Guadalcanal. Enemy bombers would be able to take off from that airstrip and bomb Allied convoys. And the Japanese would be able to use bases in the Solomons as stepping-stones from which to attack Australia. Guadalcanal had to be invaded before the Japanese could complete the airstrip. But Australian troops were either battling the Japanese in New Guinea, or they were fighting in North Africa against the Germans. That left only the American 1st Marine Division. The commanders believed the Marines needed at least six months' more training. But still they were chosen to attack Guadalcanal.

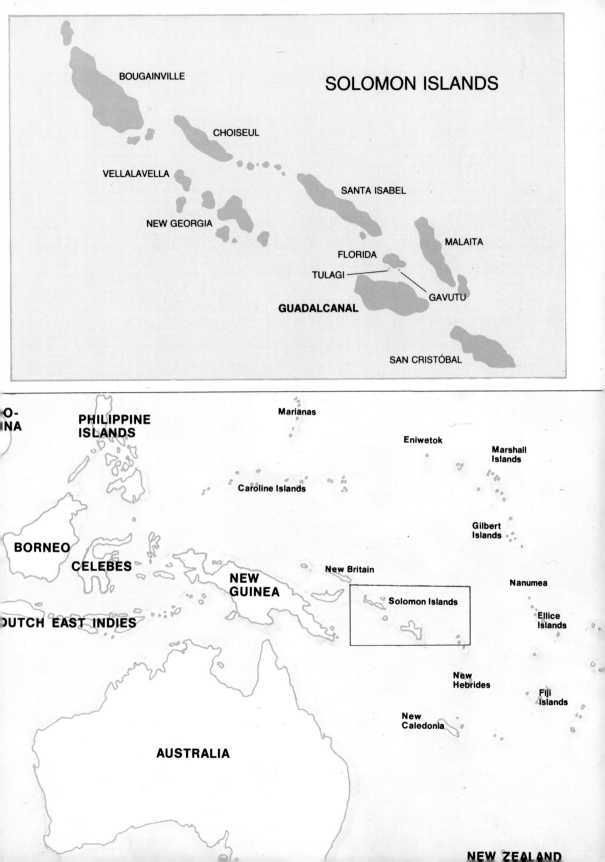

SOLOMON ISLANDS

BOUGAINVILLE

CHOISEUL

VELLALAVELLA

SANTA ISABEL

NEW GEORGIA

MALAITA

FLORIDA

TULAGI

GAVUTU

GUADALCANAL

SAN CRISTÓBAL

PHILIPPINE ISLANDS

O-INA

Marianas

Eniwetok

Marshall Islands

Caroline Islands

Gilbert Islands

BORNEO

CELEBES

NEW GUINEA

New Britain

Solomon Islands

Nanumea

DUTCH EAST INDIES

Ellice Islands

New Hebrides

Fiji Islands

New Caledonia

AUSTRALIA

NEW ZEALAND

From the air, Guadalcanal looked like a tropical paradise.

From the air or from the sea Guadalcanal looked like a tropical paradise. There were silvery beaches and mountains covered with a green mat of jungle. But the Americans quickly discovered that Guadalcanal was an island hell. The trees were laced with webs spun by spiders the size of baseballs. In between the trees stood patches of *kunai* grass whose blades could slice open a man's skin as neatly as a razor could. The jungle floor was alive with crawling

Once they had landed, the Marines discovered that Guadalcanal was an island hell.

things—nightmarish looking land crabs, beetles as big as a man's thumb, and ferocious white ants with a bite so sharp they seemed to have saw blades for jaws. Writer and world traveler Jack London once said, "If I were a king, the worst punishment I could inflict on my enemies would be to banish them to the Solomons."

Yet young Americans and young Japanese would soon die in a furious battle over this awful mound of earth.

Marines aboard a transport on their way to Guadalcanal

On August 7, 1942, eleven thousand Marines
splashed ashore on the beaches of Guadalcanal.
The invasion had caught the Japanese
completely by surprise. One hidden Japanese
radio operator saw the landing force and sent
this message: LARGE FORCE OF SHIPS. UNKNOWN
NUMBER OR TYPES. . . . WHAT CAN THEY BE? The
radio operator did not even guess they were
Americans. The Marines also landed on
the nearby islands of Tulagi, Gavutu, and
Tanambogo. There the Japanese fought brief
but stubborn battles.

On August 7, 1942, eleven thousand Marines splashed ashore on the beaches of Guadalcanal.

In their haste to escape the Americans, the Japanese left food
steaming on tables (above) and laundry drying on lines (below).

This Japanese officers' bathtub was left behind when the Japanese fled one of their camps on Guadalcanal.

In just over twenty-four hours, the Marines on Guadalcanal reached the airstrip the Japanese were building. The Japanese and Korean construction workers had fled to the hills. In their haste to escape, the workers left meals steaming on tables. They also left road graders and trucks on the field. The delighted Marines even found cases of Japanese beer and a machine that made ice.

The only casualty during the first day of the invasion of Guadalcanal came when a Marine cut his hand while trying to chop open a coconut with a bayonet.

Opposite top: An aerial view of the nearly completed runway at the airfield on Guadalcanal. Opposite bottom: Marines search for snipers in the jungle. Above: Marines use amphibious tractors to make their way through the jungle in pursuit of retreating Japanese forces.

Above: The first Japanese flag captured on Guadalcanal is held
by two American Marines. Below: This wooden building was used
as headquarters for Marine and navy fliers at Henderson Field.

Above: This Marine sits in front of his temporary home on Guadalcanal and cleans his rifle. This type of shelter was constructed by the American forces after dislodging the Japanese during the early phases of the Guadalcanal campaign. Below: Three soldiers ride a jeep over a hastily constructed bridge that spans a Guadalcanal stream.

Admiral Frank Jack Fletcher, commander of the American fleet off Guadalcanal.

But while things progressed smoothly on land, a disaster was brewing at sea.

The Allied fleet off Guadalcanal included cruisers, destroyers, and three aircraft carriers. Some of the ships were Australian. The flotilla was commanded by American Admiral Frank Fletcher. It was well known that Fletcher believed the Marines were not ready for battle and that the Japanese were very strong in this area of the Pacific. The Admiral did not want to lose his prized carriers in a battle he thought was lost before it started. He was upset that Japanese bombers were operating from bases at Rabaul on the nearby island of New Guinea.

Just two days after the landings, Fletcher withdrew his carriers from Guadalcanal waters. This left the Marines and the remaining ships unprotected from the air. That same night a Japanese fleet of seven cruisers and one destroyer sailed silently toward Guadalcanal.

For almost forty years the Japanese navy had trained its men for night attacks. In 1905 they had won a smashing victory over the Russian navy by attacking at night. To help them see at night the Japanese navy had perfected what could be called "human radar." The Japanese fleet did not have even the primitive radar of the time. So the Imperial Navy carefully tested the eyesight of every one of their sailors. Those who could see exceptionally well at night were assigned to serve as watchmen on the bows of warships. The Japanese hoped their sharp-eyed watchmen, using the excellent Japanese optical equipment, would guide their ships to victory.

Commanding the Japanese fleet was a crafty admiral named Gunichi Mikawa. He issued this final order to his commanders: "Let us go forward to certain victory in the traditional night attack of the Imperial Navy. May each one of us calmly do his utmost."

Through the darkness, a Japanese lookout spotted three Allied cruisers. Using blinker lights, Mikawa flashed out the order: PREPARE TO FIRE TORPEDOES. His ships churned to within two miles of the enemy cruisers. Incredibly, Allied sailors had not spotted the Japanese ships. And some of the Allied ships even had radar. Mikawa sent this order: ALL SHIPS ATTACK. Torpedoes splashed into the water from launching tubes. Only when the torpedoes were halfway home did the Allies realize they were under attack.

Suddenly the night turned into blazing day. Parachute flares from a Japanese float plane

Japanese bombs explode near an Australian cruiser off Guadalcanal.

exploded in the sky, casting a brilliant white
light. Searchlights flicked on and sent long
fingers of light stretching over the waters.
Heavy naval guns opened fire. Orange blasts
from muzzles popped like giant flashbulbs. The
roar of explosions sounded like thunder. Finally
came the most sickening roar of all. Torpedoes,
each one weighing more than a thousand
pounds, crashed into the sides of Allied ships.
Water and flames erupted into the night sky.
Sailors heard the screams of their wounded and
dying shipmates.

The American heavy cruiser *Chicago* (right) was hit by Japanese shells during the attack by the Japanese fleet.

The Australian ship *Canberra* and the American cruiser *Chicago* were the first to be hit. The *Canberra* burst into flames. Horribly burned sailors dashed madly about the deck. The fire from the *Canberra* lit up the *Chicago*. Japanese guns opened fire. The *Chicago* tried to fire back, but shells tore into her. Admiral Mikawa ordered his ships forward. There were still more targets to hit. Mikawa's guns and torpedoes plastered the cruisers *Astoria* and *Vincennes*. The sea became an inferno. The once black night was now lit up with fires from burning hulks of ships.

The sea battle lasted only forty minutes. The Japanese had not lost one ship. The Allied fleet was a shambles. Four modern heavy cruisers were either sunk or sinking. A later casualty count would total 1,023 American and Australian sailors dead. Hundreds more were wounded, badly burned, or desperately swimming about in the shark-infested waters. The battle had been bloody, confusing, and terrifying. It was also one of the most humiliating losses the American navy had ever suffered at sea.

The crushing defeat left the Marines on land at the mercy of the Japanese navy and air force. Marine General Alexander A. Vandegrift decided he had to dig in and protect what little territory he had—the airstrip and the beachhead. If the Japanese wanted the rest of the island they could keep it. Vandegrift realized that from now on he would have to fight a defensive war.

General Alexander A. Vandegrift (right), commander of the Marines who stormed onto Guadalcanal, plans operations with Rear Admirial R.K. Turner of the navy, who led the transport force used in the landings.

Guadalcanal was a strange battle for the United States Marines. In later battles, Marines would storm Japanese strongholds and fight battles that were bloody but brief. The Battle of Guadalcanal was bloody, but it stretched over six long months. In the future, the Marines would enjoy complete naval and air superiority. During much of this battle they had neither. And in future battles the Marines would have plenty of supplies. On Guadalcanal they had only the canned food left by Japanese workers. Finally, throughout the rest of World War II, the Marines were confident of victory with each new battle. But on Guadalcanal they almost lost.

This was the first United States plane to land on the captured Guadalcanal airstrip.

At once, American engineers rushed to complete the airstrip. The Americans used Japanese trucks and bulldozers to finish the job the Japanese had started. When it was completed, the Marines named the airstrip Henderson Field after a Marine pilot who had been killed during the Battle of Midway. Thirteen days after the landings, General Vandegrift stood on the airstrip and saw, as he later wrote, ". . . one of the most beautiful sights in my life—a flight of 12 SBD dive bombers." These were the first planes to land on Henderson Field. When they landed, Vandegrift said, "I was close to tears and I was not alone."

But building the airstrip had been no easy task. Every day the field had been pounded by Japanese bombers flying from bases at Rabaul. From the sea, Japanese ships had poured shell after shell into Marine positions. During these raids, the Marines hugged the bottoms of their foxholes and prayed. With no long-range guns or planes they could not fight back. Often the Marines were subjected to what was called harassment fire. Nightly they were visited by a lone bomber the Americans nicknamed "Washing Machine Charlie." The plane's engines sounded strangely like a washing machine. Its bombs seldom hit anything. The raids were designed only to keep the Marines awake at night so they would have less energy to fight.

The land battles of Guadalcanal centered around the airstrip. Both the Americans and the Japanese knew that whoever controlled Henderson Field controlled the island.

Above: Japanese bombers score a direct hit on a hangar during one of
their raids on Henderson Field. Below: American Marines salvage
a plane from a blazing hangar after a Japanese bombing raid.

The Japanese moved quickly to try to reoccupy the island. But they underestimated the Marines' strength. On August 18, 1942, a thousand Japanese soldiers landed about twenty miles from the Marine beachhead. At first, the Marines were not even aware of the landings. Commanding the Japanese was a cruel, impatient colonel named Kiyono Ichiki. His force was undermanned to begin with, but somehow Ichiki got the idea he could drive a full division of ten thousand Marines off the island with only half a regiment of Japanese soldiers. So without even waiting for the other half of his unit to arrive, Ichiki began a march through the jungle toward Henderson Field.

Marine patrols soon spotted the advancing Japanese. On one patrol was a native Solomon Island man named Jacob Vouza. The natives did not like intruders on their islands, but they disliked the Japanese more than they did the Americans. Perhaps that was because the Japanese had been the first intruders. Vouza, the island's former police chief, was a good-humored man who became friendly with

Jacob Vouza, who survived Japanese interrogation and torture, proudly displays the many medals awarded to him.

some of the Marines. One of them gave Vouza a tiny American flag as a present. On patrol, Vouza was captured by the Japanese and taken to Colonel Ichiki. The Japanese colonel discovered the American flag Vouza was carrying. He demanded information about American positions. Vouza refused to talk. He was tied to a tree, beaten, and finally bayoneted and left for dead. But Vouza was not dead. Incredibly, he chewed through his ropes, crawled back to his patrol, and reported the Japanese advance.

Marines dig in and wait for the Japanese advance.

Knowing he was about to be attacked, General Vandegrift had his men dig in and wait. Colonel Ichiki was very confident of success. After all, the Japanese army had achieved amazing victories during the first half of 1942. He led his men on a wild charge into the Marine lines. The result was a slaughter. In a brief battle, about eight hundred Japanese soldiers were killed. Those who survived melted into the jungle. One of them was Colonel Ichiki. Unable to bear defeat, he killed himself.

In mid-September, the Japanese again tried to recapture Guadalcanal. A force of six thousand crack troops landed and began a march toward Henderson Field. They were soon spotted by American scout planes.

Vandegrift had his men defend a ridge near the airstrip. To attack that ridge the Japanese would have to pass through a grassy field where there were few trees to shield them. In this spot a terrible battle called Bloody Ridge began.

It is sometimes said that those who find glory in war are those who have never seen a battlefield. The Battle of Bloody Ridge occurred on a rain-swept night. The Japanese charged into blazing machine guns and roaring cannons. Though most of them fell like tin soldiers, a few got through to the American lines. American and Japanese soldiers, using their bayonets, clashed in face-to-face, hand-to-hand combat. In the morning, bodies lay strewn over the grassy field. The battlefield stank of blood and death.

A Marine surveys "Bloody Ridge," where six hundred Japanese died.

The fighting on Guadalcanal fit into a pattern. The Americans fought stubbornly on the ground, but at sea their ships continued to be sunk. Many American navy men had little faith in the operations off the Solomons. So they were afraid to commit their best ships in a battle they thought was lost before it started. The Japanese, on the other hand, fought boldly at sea. But they continually underestimated the strength of the Americans on land. In their efforts to recapture the island, the Japanese sent in far too few troops to dislodge the Marines.

The pattern changed when two of World War II's most brilliant commanders became involved in the operations at Guadalcanal. For the Americans, the tough navy man Admiral William ("Bull") Halsey took over. For the Japanese, the military mastermind Admiral Isoroku Yamamoto assumed command. Yamamoto had planned the Japanese attack on Pearl Harbor.

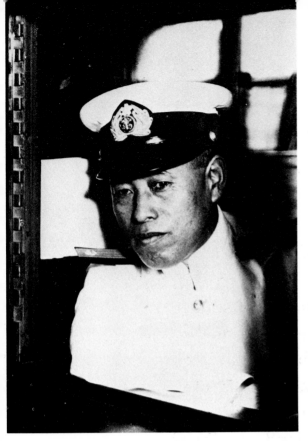

Left: Admiral Isoroku Yamamoto, commander of the Japanese Combined Fleet. Above: Admiral William ("Bull") Halsey, commander, South Pacific Area in his office.

Toward the end of 1942, both sides had decided that victory at Guadalcanal was essential. Before sailing to the island, a Japanese general named Maruyama told his men, "This is a decisive battle between Japan and the United States, a battle in which the rise or fall of the Japanese Empire will be decided."

On Guadalcanal, the many weeks in the jungle were wearing down the Marines. Flies and mosquitoes were so thick the men had to develop a special way to eat. They speared a

During lulls in the fighting, Marines kept up with the news from home (above), stood in chow lines (below), and even managed to get in a card game (right).

forkful of food from their K-ration cans, shook
the fork vigorously to drive away the flies, and
plunged the forkful into their mouths. Often
they still had to spit out a final stubborn fly. All
night long the men were tormented by buzzing
mosquitoes. Some of the mosquitoes carried the
dreaded disease malaria. A man with malaria
was stricken with awful fevers and felt as if he
were roasting one minute and freezing the next.
Tropical diseases produced more American
casualties than Japanese bombs and bullets.
With no effective cure, many Americans on
Guadalcanal died of malaria.

All over the hot, humid, hated, jungle-covered island of Guadalcanal
were scummy swamps where disease-carrying mosquitoes bred.

The battleship *South Dakota*, shown here at launching ceremonies in June of 1941, went into action in the waters off Guadalcanal.

To the military high command, though, the hellhole called Guadalcanal was an important piece of real estate. Admiral Yamamato, still smarting from his defeat at Midway, was determined to succeed at Guadalcanal. He decided to transport an entire division of troops to the island. First he sent a powerful fleet that included three carriers and two battleships. Also into the waters off the Solomons sailed an American fleet. Under the overall command of Admiral Halsey, the Americans finally sent a sufficient number of ships into action. In the American fleet were the carriers *Enterprise* and *Hornet* and the spanking new battleship *South Dakota*.

In October and November, the two navies fought a series of pitched battles. In one of those battles two huge battleships slugged it out broadside to broadside. It was a contest much like the naval battles that had been fought one hundred years earlier. But most of the battles were carrier-plane duels in which the two fleets never came within sight of each other. A Japanese admiral named Tanaka remembered one battle as a day "of carrier bombers roaring toward targets as though to plunge full in the water, releasing bombs and pulling out barely in time; each miss sending up towering columns of mist and spray; every hit raising clouds

Japanese bombers are shown as they came in low at Guadalcanal to attack United States transports (far left).

A flaming Japanese bomber (top center) heads toward
the United States carrier *Hornet* in a suicide dive.

of smoke and fire as transports burst into
flame. . . . Attacks depart, smoke screens lift,
and the tragic scene of men jumping overboard
from burning, sinking ships."

On both sides thousands of men lost their
lives and dozens of ships were sunk in the
desperate sea battles. The United States lost
the carrier *Hornet*. The Japanese lost two
battleships. But the American navy was able to
reinforce the Marines by bringing in an army
unit. And they prevented the Japanese from
landing as many troops on Guadalcanal as
Admiral Yamamoto had wanted.

The Japanese plane crashed into the *Hornet*'s signal bridge, setting the warship afire.

Still the Japanese had more soldiers on Guadalcanal than they ever had before. The soldiers were supported by light tanks and powerful 150mm cannons. Painfully, the Japanese soldiers cut roads through the jungle. Over the roads they hauled their cannons and other heavy equipment. The jungle was as much an enemy to the Japanese as it was to the Americans. The Japanese also lost more men to tropical diseases than they did to bullets.

Marines rested briefly during their march to meet the Japanese forces.

Finally the two forces met. A battle took place near the grassy field at Bloody Ridge. Troops on both sides were sick, exhausted, and frightened. Yet they closed for still more combat. The months in the jungle and the constant terror and tension of war drove some men to heroics. It drove others insane.

Marine Sergeant Mitchell Paige won the Congressional Medal of Honor for his actions during one of the last ground battles of Guadalcanal. In his words: ". . . I was so wound up I couldn't stop. . . . I picked up the machine gun, and without hardly noticing the burning hot jacket, cradled it in my arms and threw two belts of ammo over my shoulder. . . . We fired on until we reached the edge of the clearing and then there was nothing left to fire at. I was soaked and steam was rising from my gun. My hand felt funny. I looked down and saw a blister running from my fingertips to my forearm." The sergeant had scorched the skin of his arm on a hot machine-gun barrel. But he was so caught up in the fighting he had hardly noticed the pain.

When the smoke cleared, the Americans had won another victory on the ground. The island of Guadalcanal was theirs.

During the dark nights that followed, in early February of 1943, the Japanese navy evacuated about 13,000 of their troops. They were all that was left of the 36,000 soldiers who had come to fight on Guadalcanal. Some of those men were stragglers from the very first Japanese counteroffensive more than six months earlier. They had been living on roots, berries, and tree bark. One of those survivors scribbled in his diary: "We are nothing but skin and bones, pale wild men. I have become like a primitive man." The Japanese soldiers who were lucky enough to be evacuated would forever call Guadalcanal the "Isle of Death."

The Americans had lost 4,123 men. Ground forces alone suffered 1,592 dead. Many were buried in graveyards alongside the battlefields.

Throughout the world, graveyards and battlefields are found side by side. For thousands of years men have dug graves near the places where they fought battles. Wars cause territory to change hands. But the graveyards near the battlefields always remain.

The Marine graveyard at Guadalcanal was marked
with simple wooden crosses and palm fronds.

Before they left Guadalcanal, the Americans
decorated the graves of their buddies. Over the
long rows of crosses and stars they left signs
saying: "Our Buddy," "Always a Friendly
Guy," "A big guy with a bigger heart." Over
one grave is this poem:

And when he goes to heaven
To St. Peter he'll tell:
Another Marine reporting sir,
I've served my time in hell.

Victory finally theirs, these exhausted Marines
are leaving the hated island of Guadalcanal.

Index

About the Author

Mr. Stein was born and grew up in Chicago. At eighteen he enlisted in the Marine Corps where he served three years. He was a sergeant at discharge. He later received a B.A. in history from the University of Illinois and an M.F.A. from the University of Guanajuato in Mexico.

Although he served in the Marines, Mr. Stein believes that wars are a dreadful waste of human life. He agrees with a statement once uttered by Benjamin Franklin: "There never was a good war or a bad peace." But wars are all too much a part of human history. Mr. Stein hopes that some day there will be no more wars to write about.